William F. Sherwin

Portfolio of Sunday School Songs

William F. Sherwin

Portfolio of Sunday School Songs

ISBN/EAN: 9783337265410

Printed in Europe, USA, Canada, Australia, Japan

Cover: Foto ©Lupo / pixelio.de

More available books at **www.hansebooks.com**

THE
PORTFOLIO

OF

SUNDAY SCHOOL SONGS

BY

W. F. SHERWIN AND C. C. CASE

FLEMING H. REVELL

CHICAGO | NEW YORK
148 AND 150 MADISON ST. | 148 AND 150 NASSAU ST.

Publisher of Evangelical Literature.

IT IS IMPOSSIBLE

To crowd into the limits of a volume of this size all that is desirable in a book of Sunday School Song, so that all tastes shall be gratified and every requirement be met. The editors of THE PORTFOLIO have sought to compile a work which should fairly meet the demand for such hymns and music as should lend a fresh interest to the service, and give it a new impetus in an upward direction.

Their wide experience leads them to believe that the average Sunday Schools in our land will not longer tolerate that which is puerile and meaningless in hymnology, or frivolous in music, and that, on the other hand, they will quite generally be repelled by a scholastic dignity which involves much difficulty in execution.

It is hoped that a thorough and candid examination of THE PORTFOLIO may show it to contain abundance of material, in song and responsive exercises, which will at once engage the interest of all and lift the service to a higher plane.

W. F. SHERWIN.
C. C. CASE.

Copyright, 1887, by F. H. REVELL.

THE PORTFOLIO

OF

SUNDAY SCHOOL SONGS.

3. One Sweetly Solemn Thought.

PHŒBE CARY.
C. C. CASE.

Slowly.

1. One sweet - ly sol - emn thought Comes to me o'er and o'er,
2. Near - er my Fa - ther's house, Where ma - ny man - sions be;
3. Near - er the bound of life, Where bur - dens are laid down;
4. Be near me when my feet Are slip - ping o'er the brink;

I'm near - er home to - day Than I have been be - fore.
Near - er the great white throne, Near - er the jas - per sea.
Near - er to leave the cross, And near - er to the crown.
For I am near - er home, Per - haps, than now I think.

CHORUS.

Near - er my home, Near - er my home,
Near-er my home, Near - er my home,

After last verse repeat chorus pp.

Near - er my home to - day Than I have been be - fore.

(5)

5. The Lord's Day.

R. N. T.   LEWIS EDSON.

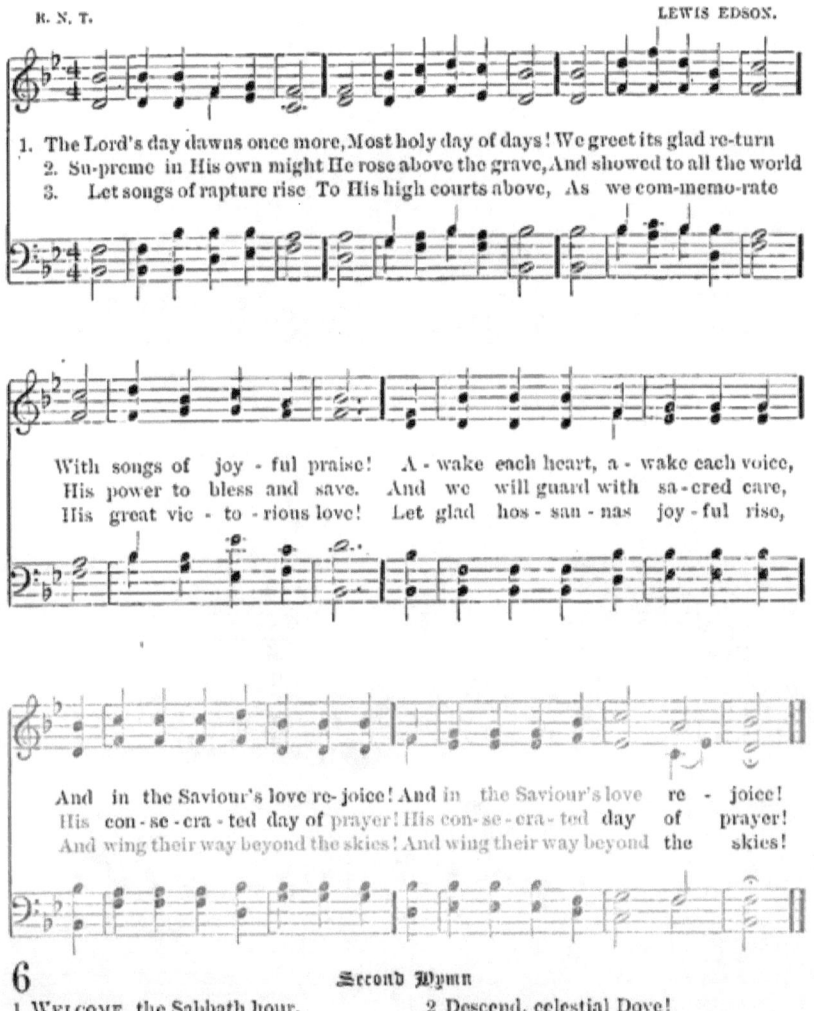

1. The Lord's day dawns once more, Most holy day of days! We greet its glad re-turn
2. Su-preme in His own might He rose above the grave, And showed to all the world
3. Let songs of rapture rise To His high courts above, As we com-mem-o-rate

With songs of joy - ful praise! A - wake each heart, a - wake each voice,
His power to bless and save. And we will guard with sa - cred care,
His great vic - to - rious love! Let glad hos - san - nas joy - ful rise,

And in the Saviour's love re-joice! And in the Saviour's love re - joice!
His con - se - cra - ted day of prayer! His con - se - cra - ted day of prayer!
And wing their way beyond the skies! And wing their way beyond the skies!

6. Second Hymn

1 WELCOME, the Sabbath hour,
   The holy and the blest!
With sweet, subduing power
   It calms the soul to rest;
And hope and love spring up anew,
To cheer us on our journey through.

2 Descend, celestial Dove!
   E'en while we wait and sing;
Come from the throne of love,
   With healing on thy wing;
With ardent zeal each heart inspire,
And rebaptize with holy fire.

HARRIET N. SMITH.

(7)

8. Only Christ.

ELIZA M. SHERMAN. C. C. CASE.

1. Je-sus Christ is all my song, And His love my sto-ry,
2. Christ a-lone is all my hope, He my Rock of A-ges,
3. Christ a-lone shall be my trust, Je-sus my sal-va-tion;

While His pre-cious prom-is-es Form my crown of glo-ry.
He my ref-uge from the storm When the tem-pest ra-ges.
He my rock and right-eous-ness, And my sure foun-da-tion.

REFRAIN.

Christ a-lone, ... Christ a-lone, ...
Christ a-lone, Christ a-lone,
From Him naught can sev-er, I will praise for-ev-er.

4
Other refuge have I none,
While He's interceding;
Christ alone shall be my plea,
And His love my pleading.

14. The Master's Call.

FANNY CROSBY.   W. F. SHERWIN. By per.

1. The Mas-ter is come, and calleth for thee, He stands at the door of thy heart; No
2. The Mas-ter has come with blessings for thee, Arise, and His message receive: Thy
3. The Master is come, and calleth thee now, This moment what joy may be thine; How
4. He waits for thee still, then haste with delight, Oh, fly to the arms of His love; Press

friend so for-giv-ing, so gen-tle as He, Oh, say, wilt thou let Him de-part?
ran-som is purchased, thy par-don is free, If thou wilt re-pent and be-lieve.
ten-der the smile that il-lumines His brow, A pledge of His fa-vor di-vine.
on to that beau-ti-ful mansion of light, Prepared in His kingdom a-bove.

REFRAIN.
Patiently wait-ing, earnestly plead-ing, Jesus, thy Saviour, knocks at thy heart;
Patiently wait-ing,

Patiently wait-ing, earnestly pleading, Jesus, thy Saviour knocks at thy heart.
wait-ing, plead-ing,

(15)

Jesus, Lover of my Soul.

2 Other refuge have I none;
 Hangs my helpless soul on Thee;
Leave, oh, leave me not alone,
 Still support and comfort me.
All my trust on Thee is stayed;
 All my help from Thee I bring;
Cover my defenceless head
 With the shadow of Thy wing.

3 Thou, O Christ, art all I want;
 More than all in Thee I find;
Raise the fallen, cheer the faint,
 Heal the sick, and lead the blind.

Just and holy is Thy name,
 I am all unrighteousness;
Vile and full of sin I am,
 Thou art full of truth and grace.

4 Plenteous grace with Thee is found,
 Grace to cover all my sin;
Let the healing stream abound.
 Make me, keep me, pure within;
Thou of life the Fountain art,
 Freely let me take of Thee;
Spring Thou up within my heart,
 Rise to all eternity.

16. Bless Our School To-day.

H. A. LEWIS.

1. Je-sus, ten-der Sav-iour, Bless our school to-day,
   While we sing Thy prais-es, While we hum-bly pray,
   On this bless-ed Sab-bath, May our hearts be stirred
   By the faith-ful teach-ings Of Thy ho-ly Word.

2. Lead us, ten-der Sav-iour, In the nar-row way;
   Help us all to love Thee, And Thy truth o-bey.
   Own the praise we bring Thee, Hear us when we pray;
   Make us Thy dear chil-dren, Bless our school to-day.

22. Grant Thy Blessing, Lord.

STUDY SONG.

W. F. S.   W. F. S.

1. Grant Thy bless-ing now, O Lord, While we look in - to Thy word;
To our hearts Thy truth re - veal; Fill us with a ho - ly zeal.
2. Ho - ly Spir - it, now in - spire Every thought and all de - sire;
Fix our minds on things a - bove, Stir a - new the fires of love.
3. Sanc - ti - fy us, Lord, we pray, By the les - sons of this day;
May our souls by Thee be fed, And to liv - ing fountains led.

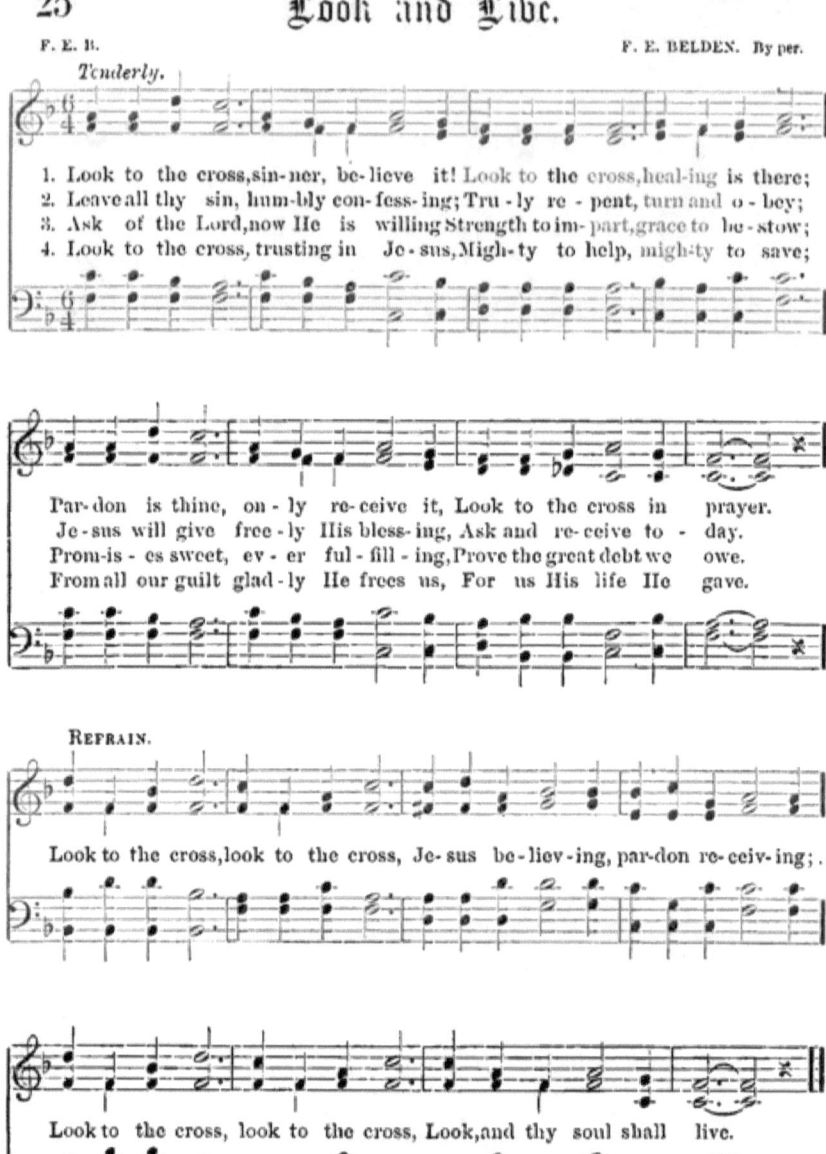

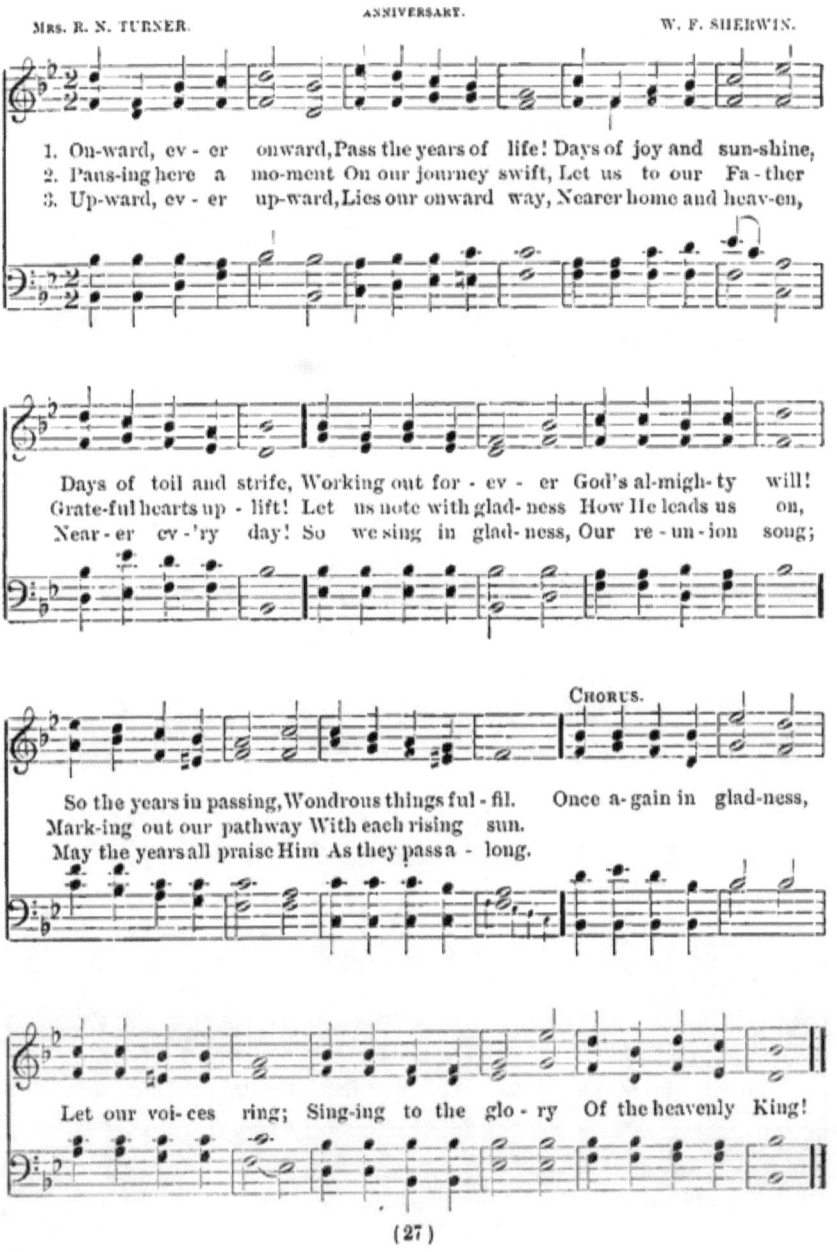

34. He's Coming Soon.

Copyright, 1886, by F. E. Belden.

37. Feast of the King.

Mrs. R. N. Turner. Feb. 19, 1885.
T. Martin Towne.

Duet for Soprano and Alto.

1. "I o-pen wide my door be-loved, And bid you en-ter in to share The choic-est ban-quet of my house Pre-pared for you with lov-ing care!
2. "Let not the triv-ial things of life, Employ your heart and hand to-day, But leave all else, and with glad soul To me your grate-ful hom-age pay!

Quartet.

"Oh, turn ye not a-side from me And slight the proffered feast I give, Draw
"My feast is spread, I bid you come, O well-be-lov-ed ones and true; My

We come, for Thou, O gra-cious One, Wilt cleanse our souls from ev-ery sin—The

Chorus. (For the whole school after last verse.)

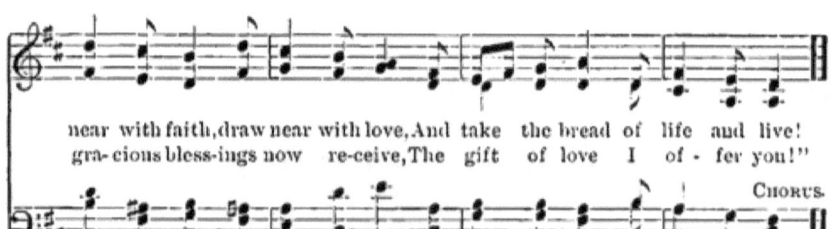

near with faith, draw near with love, And take the bread of life and live!
gra-cious bless-ings now re-ceive, The gift of love I of-fer you!"

Chorus.

ho-ly robe of Thy dear love Shall make us meet to en-ter in.

38. Even at the Door.

F. E. B.
F. E. BELDEN. By per.

1. The com-ing King is at the door Who once the cross for sin-ners bore,
2. The signs that show His coming near Are fast ful-fill-ing year by year,
3. Look not on earth for strife to cease, Look not be-low for joy and peace,
4. Then in the glorious earth made new We'll dwell the countless a-ges through;

But now the right-eous ones a - lone He comes to gath-er home.
And soon we'll hail the glo-rious dawn Of heav'n's e - ter - nal morn.
Un - til the Sav-iour comes a - gain To ban-ish death and sin.
This mor-tal shall im - mor - tal be, Through all e - ter - ni - ty.

CHORUS.

At the door, at the door, At the door, yes, e - ven at the door;
At the door, at the door,

He is com - ing, He is com - ing, He is e - ven at the door.
com-ing a - gain, com-ing a - gain,

Copyright, 1886, by F. E. BELDEN.

39. Love Divine.

Mrs. M. O. PAGE.   C. C. CASE.

1. There's a world of love a-waiting Ev-ery pil-grim that may be Press-ing onward toward that cit-y Just be-yond the crys-tal sea. Love di-vine, this is our path-way, Love di-vine, our fount of cheer; Love di-vine will sure-ly o-pen Gates of heav'n while wait-ing here.

2. There are ros-es on the high-way, There are song birds in the vale; There's a breath of won-drous sweetness Wafted on each pass-ing gale. Love di-vine fount of cheer, Love di-vine, sure-ly o-pen Gates of heav'n while wait-ing here.

3. There are skies that nev-er dark-en, There are soft winds blow-ing sweet; There's a path-way that is fit-ted For the gen-tle pil-grim's feet.

42. Saviour, When to Thee I Flee.

Mrs. R. N. T.
W. F. S.

1. Sav-iour, when to Thee I flee, Thou my hid-ing-place wilt be;
Cov-ert strong, when foes ap-pear, Rock and Ref-uge ev-er near!
Thou art strength in ev-ery need! Thou my hun-gry soul dost feed!
Wa-ter-brooks of life im-part Cour-age to my faint-ing heart!

2. Ev-er-last-ing is the Arm That de-fends me from all harm;
Here I rock my soul to rest Safe up-on my Sav-iour's breast!
While I draw life's eag-er breath, Till all strug-gles close in death,
Shield me, Ref-uge from a-bove, Shield me 'neath Thy wings of love.

50. Rejoice in Christ.

H. H. W. EDMANDS. W. F. SHERWIN.

1. Re-joice! re-joice in Christ our Lord! The King of beau-ty He!
   With maj-es-ty and might a-dorned, And glorious lib-er-ty.
   Re-joice! re-joice in grace so free, So full of beau-ty,—we
   Ac-cord to Him, our conquering Lord, A glo-rious fe-al-ty.

2. Re-joice! re-joice! sin reigns no more Our mas-ter still to be:—
   Love rends the chain that held us down And ends mor-tal-i-ty.
   Re-joice! re-joice we'll rest at last Where Christ shall ev-er be;
   A-way from sin, and death, and fear, In im-mor-tal-i-ty.

Christ My Joy.

C. C. CASE.

1. Christ, of all my hopes the ground, Christ, the spring of all my joy,
2. Firm-ly trust-ing in Thy blood, Noth-ing shall my heart con-found;

Still in Thee let me be found, Still for Thee my powers em-ploy:
Safe-ly I shall pass the flood, Safe-ly reach Im-manuel's ground.

Foun-tain of o'er-flow-ing grace. Free-ly from Thy full-ness give:
When I touch the bless-ed shore, Back the clos-ing waves shall roll;

Till I close my earth-ly race, Be it "Christ for me to live."
Death's dark stream shall nev-er more Part from Thee my rav-ished soul.

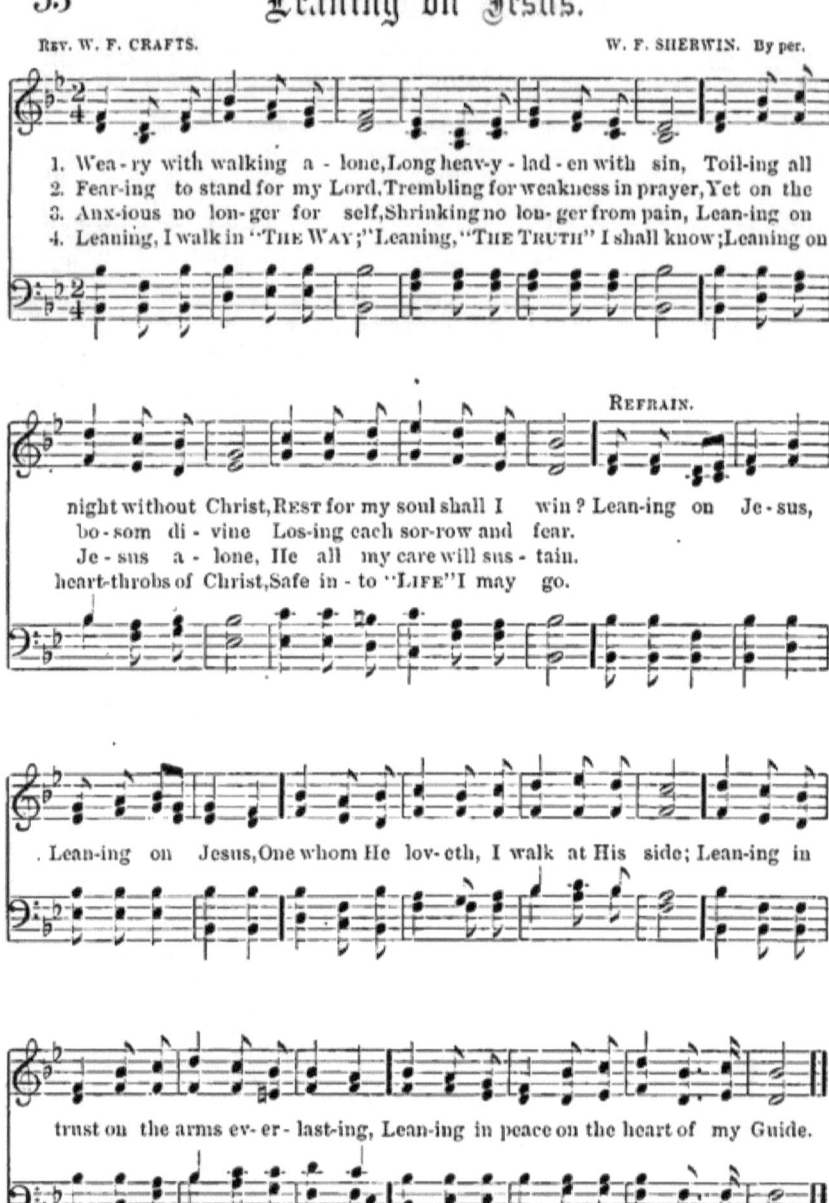

57. My Strong Salvation.

JAMES MONTGOMERY. — Rev. T. R. MATTHEWS.

1. God is my strong salvation, What foe have I to fear?
   In darkness and temptation, My Light, my Help is near;
   Though hosts encamp around me, Firm to the fight I stand;
   What terror can confound me, With God at my right hand?

2. Place on the Lord reliance; My soul! with courage wait;
   His truth be thine affiance When faint and desolate;
   His might thy heart shall strengthen, His love thy joy increase;
   Mercy thy days shall lengthen; The Lord will give thee peace.

58. For God and Duty.

Mrs. R. N. TURNER.   W. F. SHERWIN.

1. Christ is calling us to action, Faithful fol-l'wers ev-'ry one; Urging us to earnest effort Ere the setting of the sun.
2. Fear not thou, but still press onward, Christ's own hand points out the way! Inward foes to meet in battle, Sinful tho'ts to fight and slay!
3. For His sake, thou must be willing That thy light may shine abroad, Leading some that may be straying, To the joy and peace of God!
4. Earnest effort, true and patient, Thou must make for God and man; So fulfilling, strong and willing, Ev'ry day thy Father's plan!

CHORUS.
Wake! oh, wake for God and duty! Gird the gospel armor on; With the cross of Christ to lead you, Full of courage, follow on!

59. Return, O Wanderer!

C. C. CASE.

1. Return, O wanderer, now return, And seek thy Father's face!
Those new desires which in thee burn, Were kindled by His grace.

2. Return, O wanderer, now return, Thy Saviour bids thee live;
Go to His bleeding feet, and learn How freely He'll forgive.

3. Return, O wanderer, now return, And wipe the falling tear!
Thy Father calls; no longer mourn: His love invites thee near.

Solo. Return, O wand'rer, now return, And seek, and seek thy Father's face. Return, O wand'rer, now return, And seek thy Father's face.

Return, O wand'rer, now return, And seek thy Father's, Father's face. Return, O wand'rer, now return, And seek, and seek thy Father's face.

now return, And seek thy Father's face.

61. Marching On.

W. F. S.
W. F. SHERWIN.

March movement.

1. Marching on with shout and song, Gathers now a mighty throng; See the banners brightly gleaming in the morning light! We're the army of the Lord, And our weapon is the Word. Jesus Christ is our Commander; we can trust His might. We have heard the trumpet call, Pealing out to one and all With its warning to awake and put the gospel armor on.

2. Will you join our ranks to-day, And the heav'nly call obey? Come, enlist against the surging hosts of sin and shame. Tho' there may be toil and strife, You shall win eternal life, For the world shall yet be conquer'd in the Saviour's name. Then we'll all go marching on Till the victory is won; Only in the day of triumph may we lay our armor down.

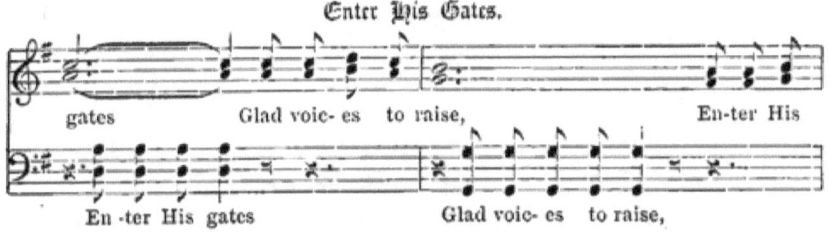

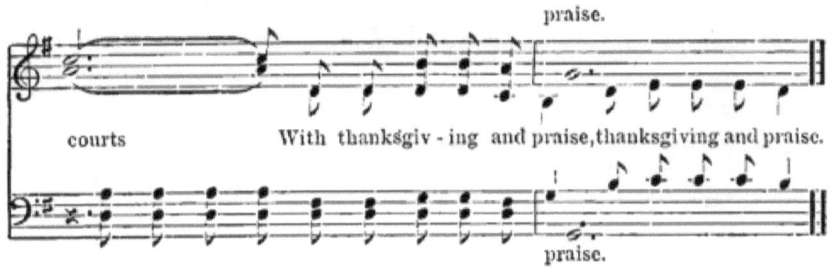

67. Jott. 8s & 7s.

C. C. CASE.

1. Yes, for me, for me He careth With a brother's tender care;
2. Yes, o'er me, o'er me He watcheth, Ceaseless watcheth night and day;
3. Yes, for me He standeth pleading At the mercy-seat above;

Yes, with me, with me He shareth Every burden, I may bear.
Yes, e'en me, e'en me He snatcheth From the perils of the way.
Ever for me interceding, Constant in untiring love.

69 Why not To-night?

HORATIUS BONAR, D.D. W. F. S. 1887.

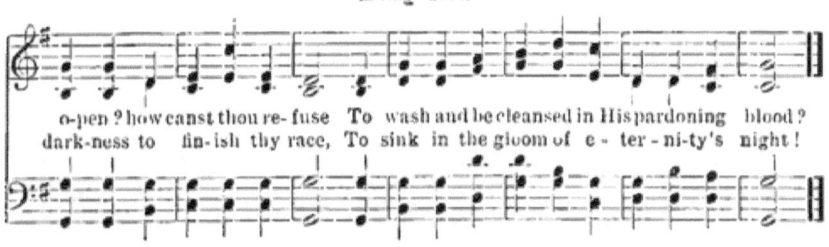

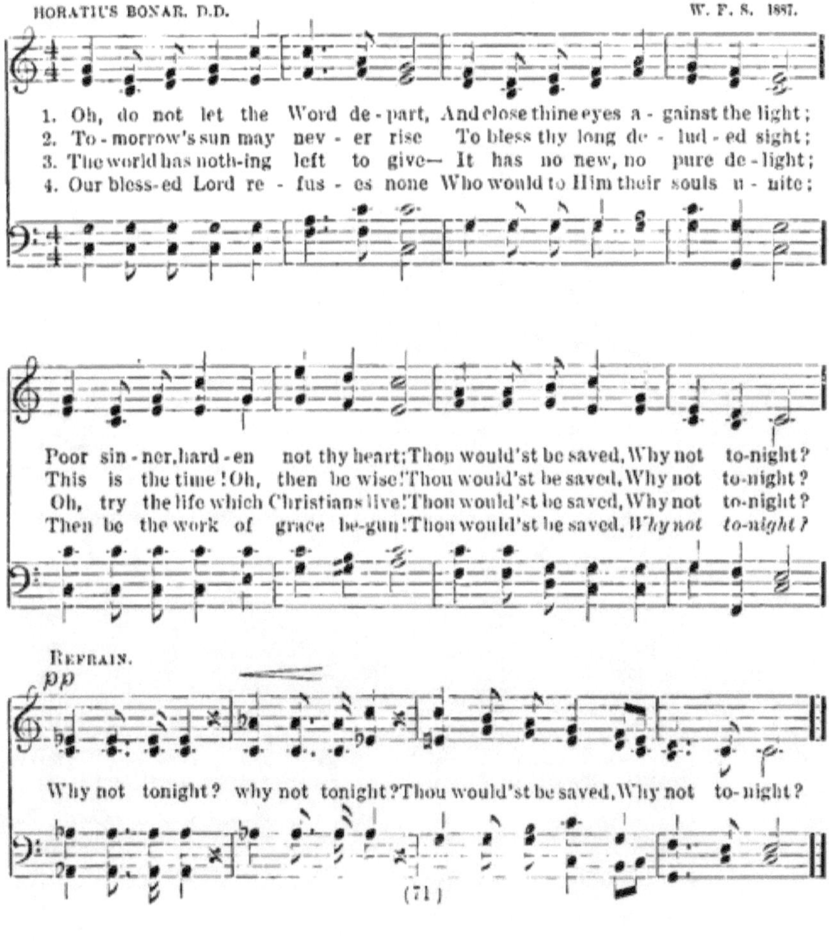

72. Tarry by the Living Waters.

F. E. B. F. E. BELDEN. By per.

1. We'll tar-ry by the liv-ing wa-ters, The fountain pure and free;
2. When wea-ry with the toilsome jour-ney, 'Tis sweet to rest a-while
3. Then come to Christ, the liv-ing wa-ter, Thy strength will He re-store;

There Je-sus waits to give us wel-come, A welcome sweet 'twill be.
Where crys-tal wa-ters gen-tly mur-mur, And sun-ny fountains smile.
Come, taste the joy of His sal-va-tion, And drink to thirst no more.

CHORUS.

We'll tar-ry by the liv-ing wa-ters, Tar-ry by the liv-ing wa-ters;
fount of liv-ing waters, fount of liv-ing waters;

Tar-ry by the liv-ing wa-ters, Tar-ry by the Fount of Life.
fount of liv-ing wa-ters,

Copyrighted 1886, by the J. E. WHITE PUB. CO.

74. Salvation! O! the Joyful Sound.

WATTS.   C. C. CASE.

1. Sal-va-tion! O! the joy-ful sound! What pleasure to our ears;
A sovereign balm for ev-ery wound, A cor-dial for our fears.

2. Sal-va-tion! let the ech-o fly The spa-cious earth a-round,
While all the ar-mies of the sky Con-spire to raise the sound.

3. Sal-va-tion! O Thou bleed-ing Lamb, To Thee the praise be-longs;
Sal-va-tion shall in-spire our hearts And dwell up-on our tongues.

CHORUS.

Sal-va-tion! O, the joy-ful! sound. A sovereign balm for ev-ery wound. Sal-va-tion! O, the joy-ful sound, A sovereign balm for ev-ery wound.

77. Safely Through Another Week.

JOHN NEWTON.   W. F. SHERWIN.

1. Safe - ly through an - oth - er week, God has brought us on our way; Let us now a bless-ing seek, Wait-ing in His courts to - day: Day of all the week the best, Em-blem of e - ter - nal rest.
2. Here we come Thy name to praise; Let us feel Thy pres-ence near; May Thy glo - ry meet our eyes, While we in Thy house ap - pear: Here af - ford us, Lord, a taste Of our ev - er - last-ing feast.
3. May Thy gos - pel's joy - ful sound Con - quer sin - ners, com - fort saints; Make the fruits of grace a - bound, Bring re - lief from all com - plaints: Thus may all our Sab-baths prove, Till we join the church a - bove.

(79)

93. What Shall I Do?

F. E. B.
F. E. BELDEN. By per.

1. What shall I do for Christ, my Saviour? How shall I pay the debt I owe?
   He has redeemed me out of bondage, What shall I do my love to show?
2. First will I tell Him I have wandered, Ask Him to take me back a-gain;
   Ask Him that I may be for-giv-en, Ask Him to take a-way my sin.
3. Then will I take the blessed Bi-ble, Searching it well, that I may be
   A-ble to help some one to love Him,—Je-sus, my Lord, who first loved me.

Chorus.

This will I do for Je-sus, my Sav-iour, This will I do my love to show:
Tell of His goodness, tell of His mer-cy, Walk in His foot-steps here be-low.

Copyrighted, 1886, by The J. E. White Pub. Co.

We are Marching Home.

H. A. LEWIS.

1. We are marching to that heav'nly home, To the dear, dear home of the blest; We shall sing a-round the ho-ly throne In that blessed land of rest.
2. We are marching to that heav'nly home, To the mansions wait-ing a-bove, Pre-par'd with-in our Father's dome, Where is on-ly joy and love.

CHORUS.

We are marching, marching home, To the New Je-ru-sa-lem, To our hap-py, hap-py home on high. We are march-ing, marching home, To the New Je-ru-sa-lem, To our hap-py, hap-py home on high.

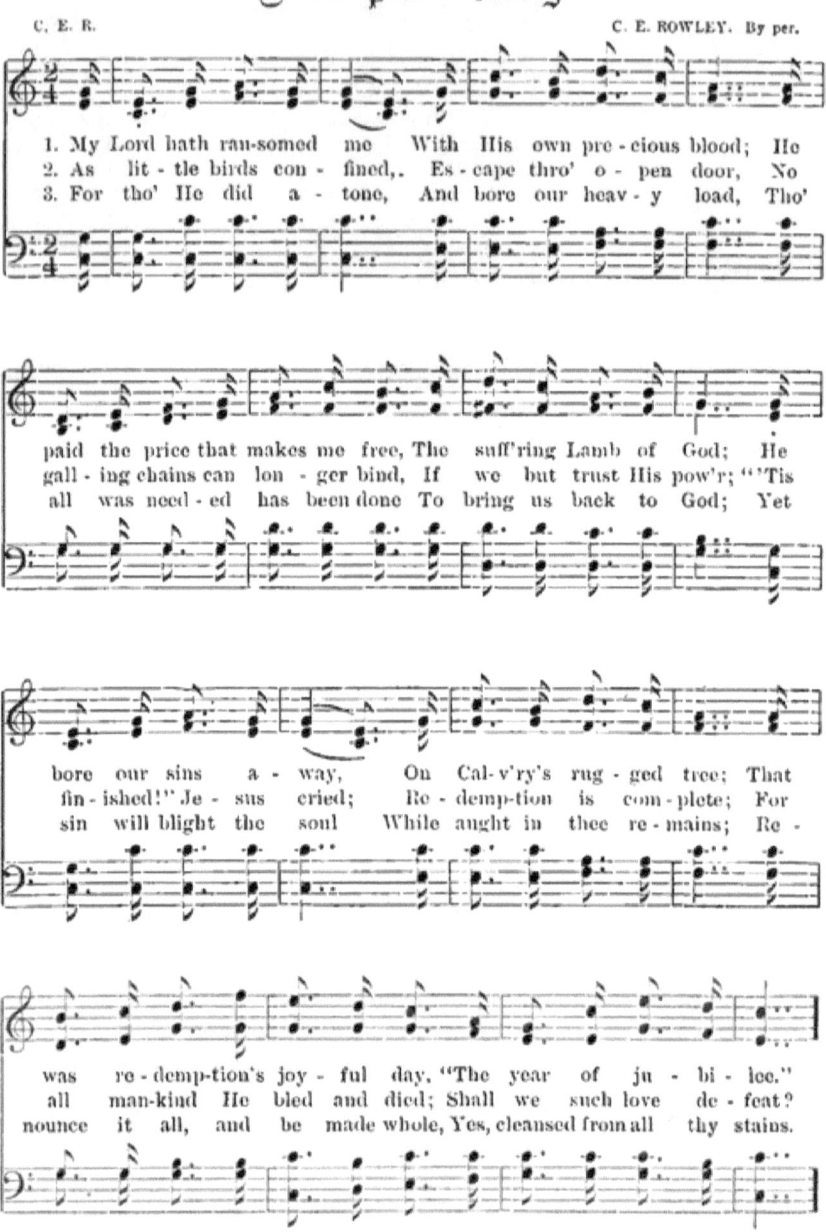

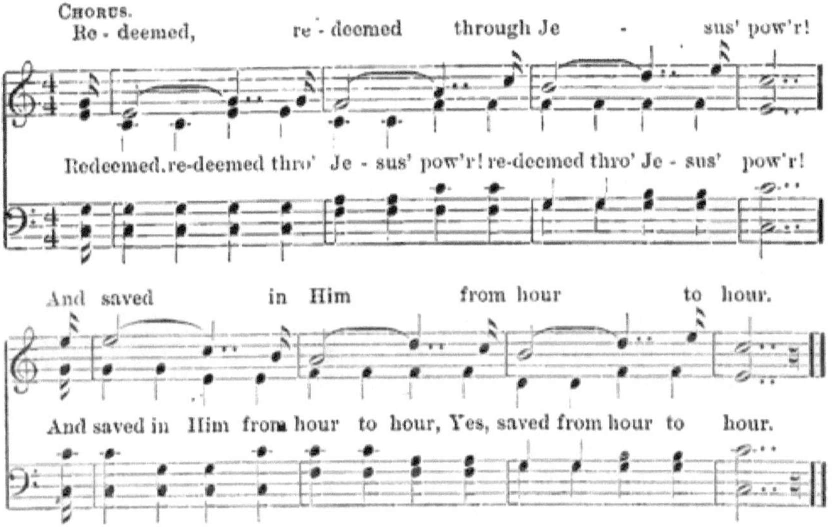

Redemption Song.

CHORUS.
Re-deemed, re-deemed through Jesus' pow'r!
And saved in Him from hour to hour.

Redeemed, re-deemed thro' Jesus' pow'r! re-deemed thro' Jesus' pow'r!
And saved in Him from hour to hour, Yes, saved from hour to hour.

99 Blest are the Pure in Heart.

J. M. BLOSE.

1. Blest are the pure in heart, For they shall see our God; The secret of the Lord is theirs; Their soul is Christ's abode.
2. The Lord, who left the heav'ns Our life and peace to bring, To dwell in lowliness with men, Their pattern and their King.
3. He to the lowly soul Doth still Himself impart, And for His dwelling and His throne, Chooseth the pure in heart.
4. Lord, we Thy presence seek; May ours this blessing be; Give us a pure and lowly heart, A temple meet for Thee.

(101)

100 The Sweet Story of Old.

(MAY BE USED AS A SOLO.)

Mrs. J. LUKE. | Arr. for this work by W. F. S.

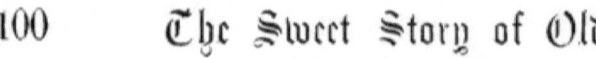

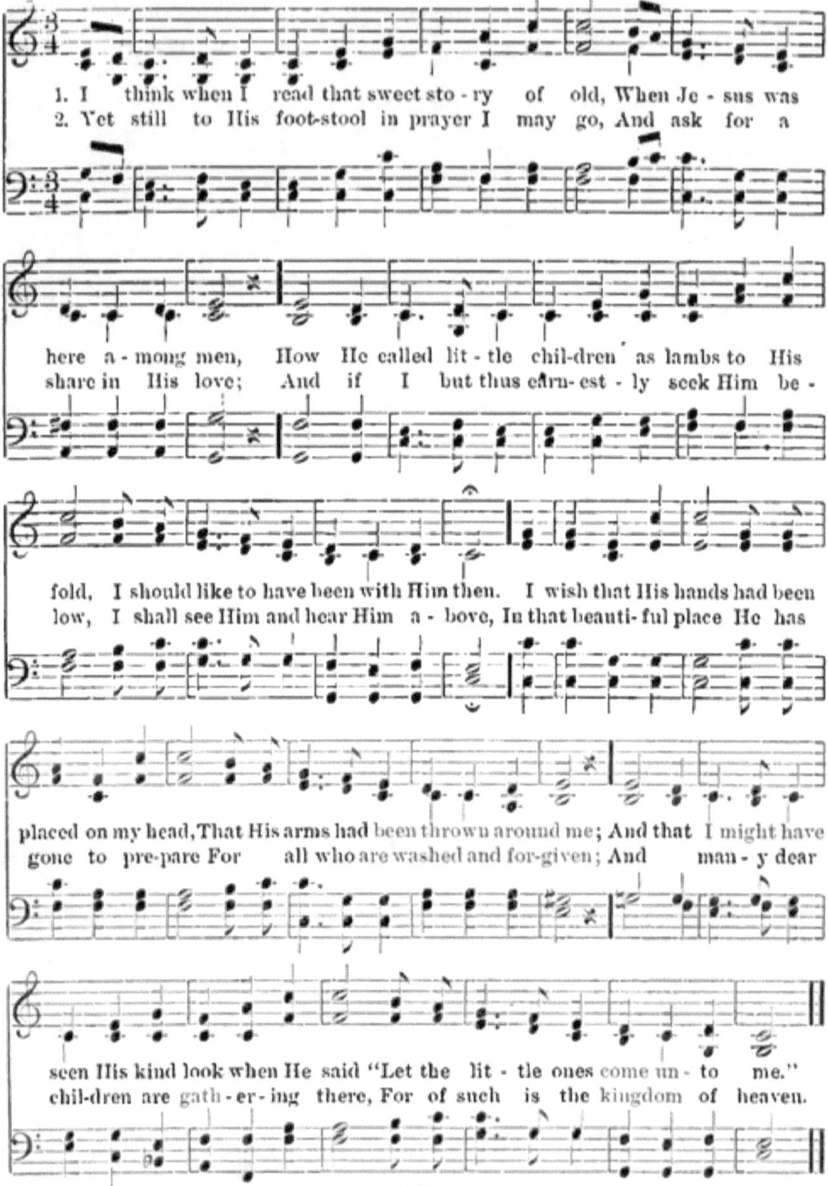

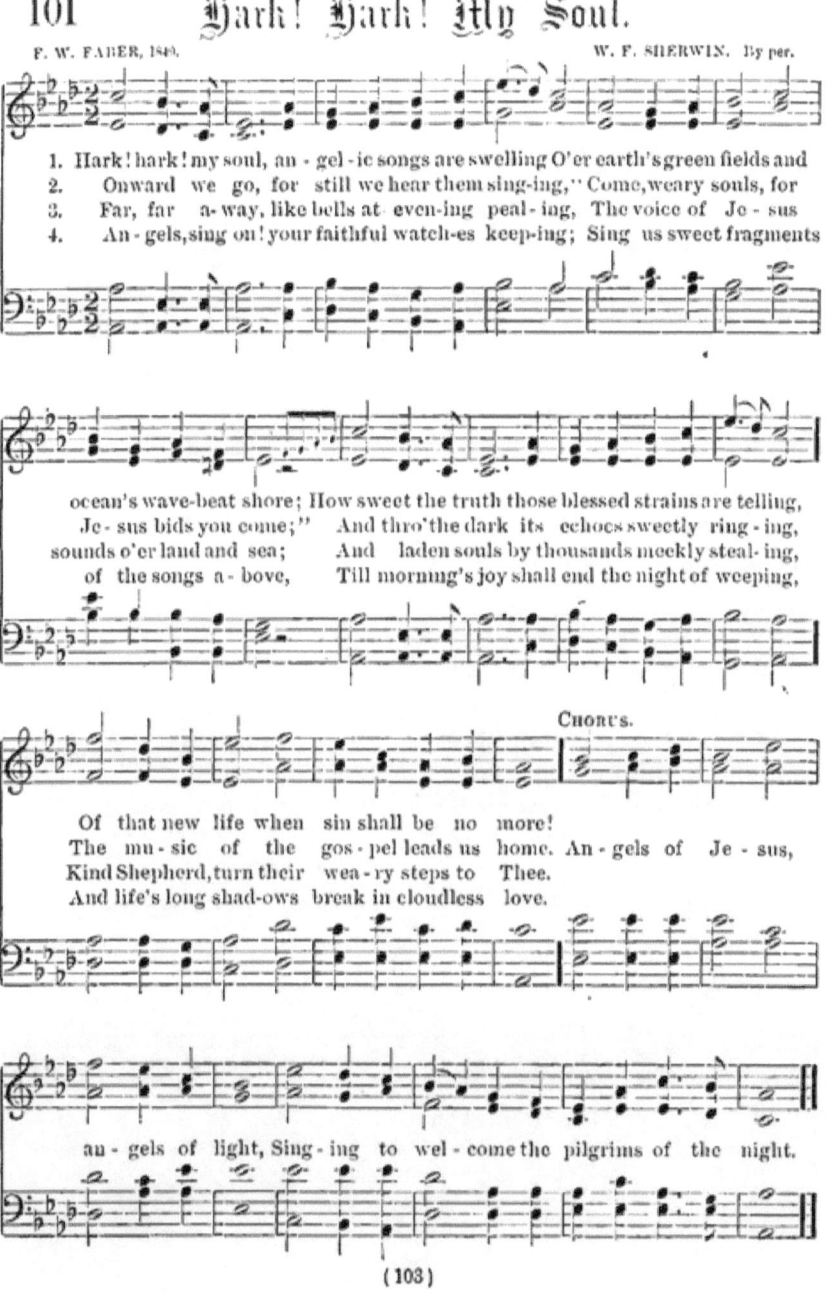

By permission, from JASPER AND GOLD.

108. How Much I Need Thee!

F. E. B.
F. E. BELDEN, By per.

1. Bless-ed Lord, how much I need Thee! Weak and sin-ful, poor and blind;
2. Clothe me with Thy robe of meekness. Stained with sin this robe of mine;
3. Safe am I if Thou dost guide me.—Trusting self, how soon I fall!
4. Then what-e'er the fu-ture bring-eth, Smiles of joy, or tears of grief,

Take my trem-bling hand and lead me: Strength and sight in Thee I find.
Teach me first to feel my weak-ness. Then to plead for strength divine.
Walk life's rug-ged way be-side me. Thou my light, my life, my all.
Still to Thee my spir-it cling-eth; Thou art still my soul's re-lief.

REFRAIN.

Ev-'ry hour, ev-'ry hour, Bless-ed Lord, how much I need Thee!
Ev-'ry hour, ev-'ry hour, Sav-iour, keep me ev-'ry hour.

Copyright, 1886, by F. E. BELDEN.

109. Chief of Sinners tho' I be.

McCOMB. F. SHERWIN.
With tender earnestness.

1. Chief of sinners though I be, Jesus shed His blood for me; Died that I might live on high, Died that I might never die; As the branch is to the vine, I am His and He is mine.
2. Oh, the height of Jesus' love! Higher than the heav'ns above, Deeper than the depths of sea, Lasting as eternity; Love that found me— wondrous tho't!—Found me when I sought Him not!
3. Chief of sinners though I be, Christ is all in all to me; All my wants to Him are known, All my sorrows are His own. Safe with Him from earthly strife, He sustains my hidden life.

114. The Accepted Time.

N. L. G.
N. L. GLOVER.

1. Tar-ry not, my broth-er, for now's th'accept-ed time. Je-sus waits your com-ing, Seek His love di-vine. Wait not for the mor-row, that may nev-er be. Give your heart to Je-sus for all e-ter-ni-ty.

2. Tar-ry not, my sis-ter, 'Tis dangerous to de-lay. Christ in-vites you, seek His love; Seek with-out de-lay. Shall we not o-bey Him, seek His love to win, When the door is o-pen, bid-ding us come in?

CHORUS.

Come, come to Je-sus. Now's th'accepted time. Je-sus waits to re-ceive you. Own and make Him thine.

(116)

116. When the Harvest is Past.

S. F. SMITH, D.D.   W. F. SHERWIN.

1. When the har-vest is past, and the sum-mer is gone, And ser-mons and prayers shall be o'er; When the beams cease to break of the blest Sabbath morn, And Je-sus in-vites thee no more— When the rich gales of mer-cy no lon-ger shall blow, The gos-pel no mes-sage de-clare— Sin-ner,

2. When the ho-ly have gone to the re-gions of peace, To dwell in the mansions a-bove; When their har-mo-ny wakes, in the ful-ness of bliss, Their song to the Sav-iour of love— Say, O sin-ner now liv-ing at rest and se-cure, And fear-ing no trou-ble to come, Can thy

(118)

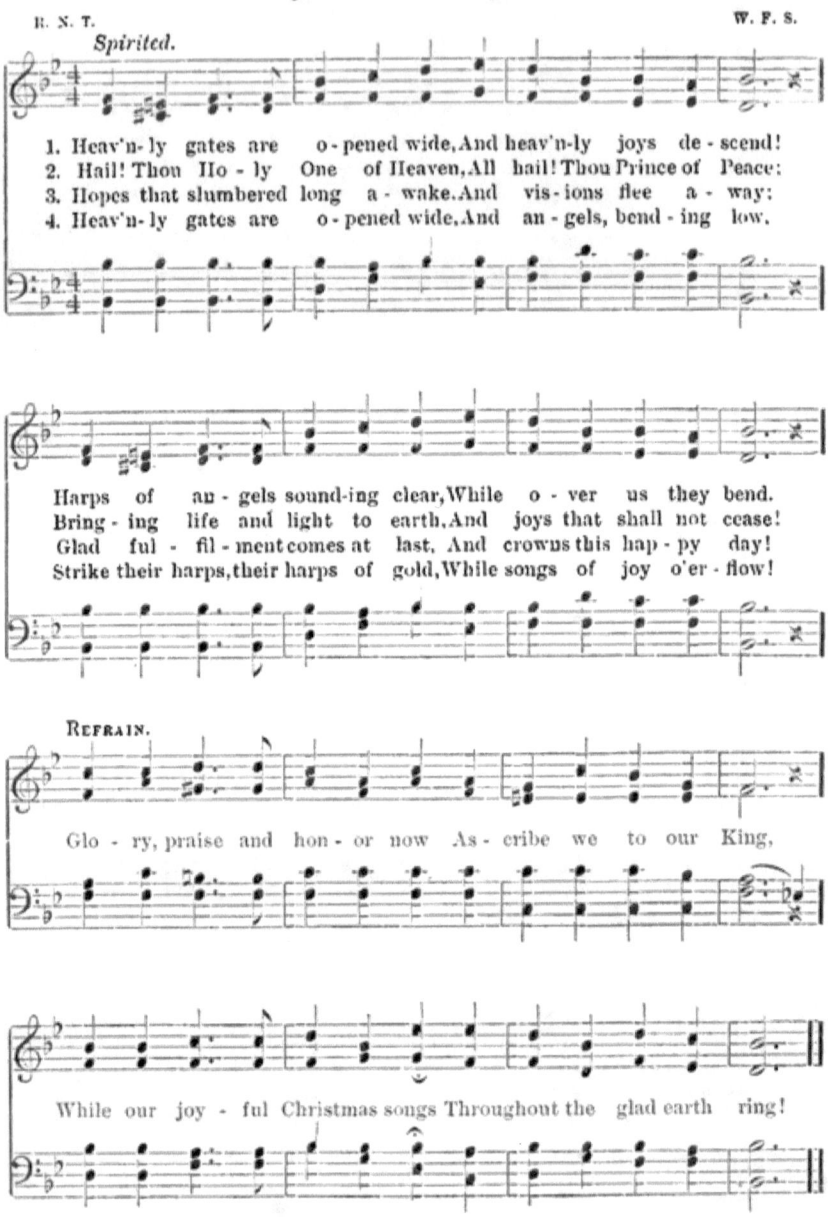

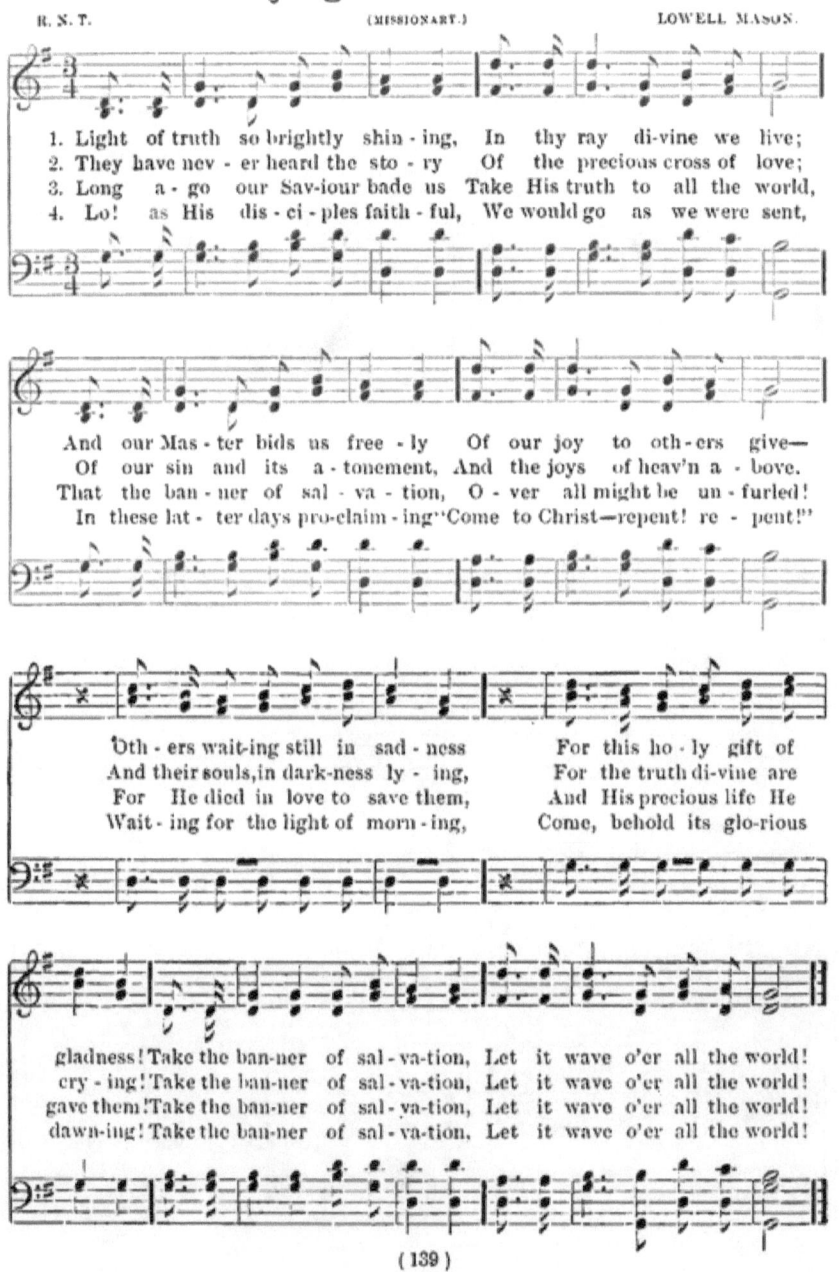

139. I Never Knew You.

Mrs. GEO. C. NEEDHAM. C. C. CASE. By per.

1. When the King, in His beau-ty, Shall come to His throne, And a-
round Him are gather'd His lov'd ones, His own. There be some who will knock at His
fair pal-ace door, To be answered with-in, "There is mer-cy no more."

2. They had known whence He came, And the grace which He brought; In their
presence He heal'd, in their streets He had tau't; They had mention'd His name and their
friendship professed, But they nev-er be-lieved, for of them He con-fessed,

3. Now the right-eous are reign-ing with A-bra-ham there, But for
these is ap-point-ed an end-less de-spair; It is vain that they call, He once
knocked at their gate; But they welcom'd Him not, so now this is their fate.

4. O lost sin-ner, be-lieve this sad sto-ry of gloom, For the
dark hour is near-ing that fix-es your doom; And I know not how long ere thy
poor breaking heart In its hor-ror shall die, as the King cries "De-part."

CHORUS.

"I have nev-er known you, I have nev-er known you;
I have nev-er, I have nev-er, I have nev-er known you."

Copyright, 1879, by C. C. Case.

141 I Love to Tell the Story.

KATE HANKEY. W. G. FISCHER.

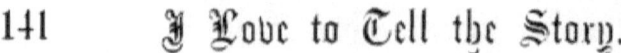

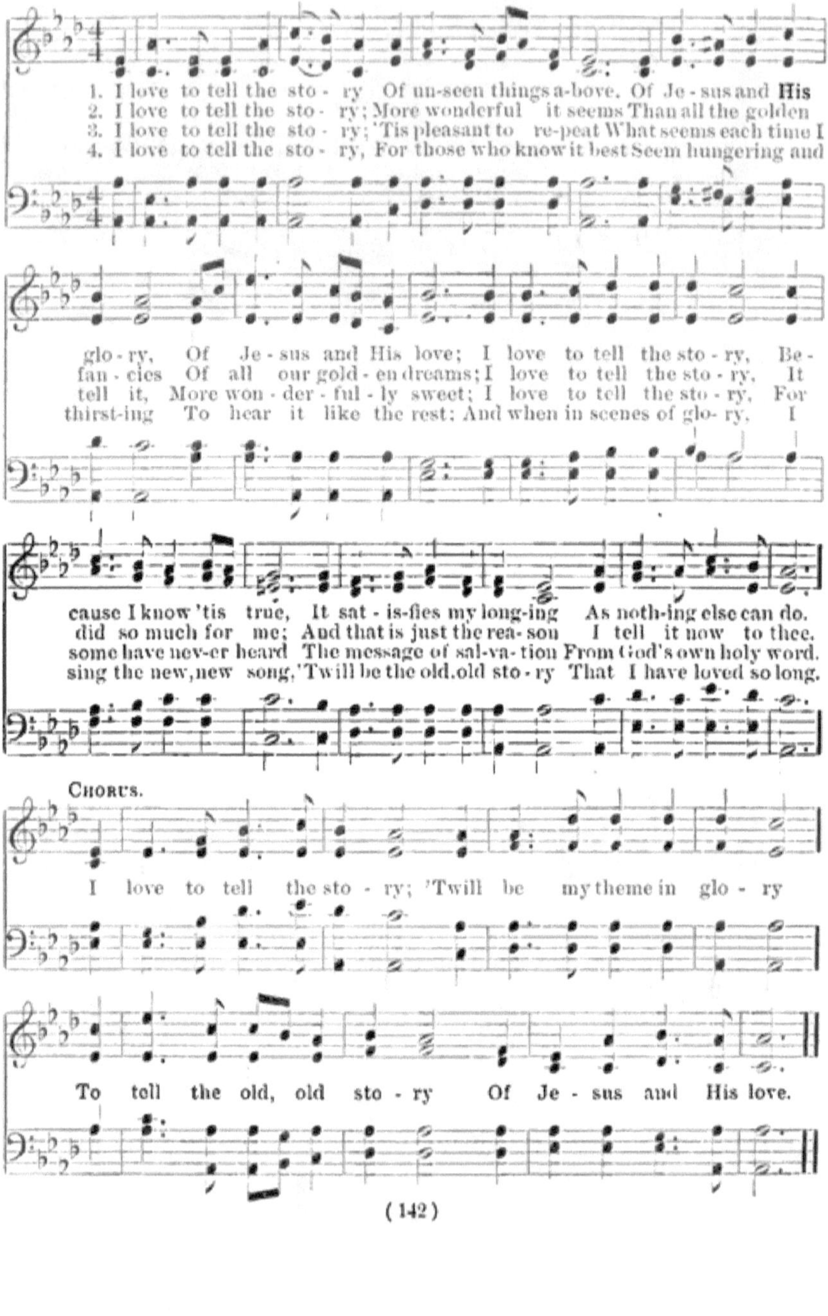

148 Tune, MARCHING THROUGH GEORGIA.

1 Come with hearts and voices now, and sing a gospel song;
 Sing it with a spirit that will move the mighty throng;
 Sing it till the world shall hear the echoes loud and long,
  While we are marching to glory!

CHORUS.—Then, hail! all hail the coming Jubilee!
 Redeemed from sin, 'tis Jesus makes us free;
 Now we'll shout salvation from the mountains to the sea,
  While we are marching to glory!

2 Gird the gospel armor on, and duty's call obey,
 See the host of Satan, ready marshalled for the fray;
 Going forth to meet them, let us watch, and fight, and pray,
  While we are marching to glory!

CHORUS.—Then hail! all hail the coming Jubilee! etc.

3 Forward, then, to battle 'neath the banner of the cross,
 Counting worldly honors, at their best, as only dross;
 Jesus is our Captain, and we ne'er can suffer loss,
  While we are marching to glory!

CHORUS.—Then, hail! all hail the coming Jubilee! etc.

4 We shall win the vic'try by the power of the *Word* ;
 This our glorious weapon—tis the Spirit's mighty sword;
 We are sure to conquer—'tis the promise of the Lord,
  For we are marching to glory!

CHORUS.—Then, hail! all hail the coming Jubilee! etc.

W. F. S. 1896.

149 Tune, SWEET HOUR OF PRAYER.

1 Obeying Thy divine behest,
 We meet, O Christ, to speak of Thee;
 Thou art amongst us as a guest;
 We feel it though we cannot see.
 We seem to breathe in glad surprise
 An atmosphere of love and bliss,
 And read within each other's eyes
 To whom it is we owe all this.

2 O let us, then, dear Lord, be blest
 With Thy sweet presence every day;
 Be with us as our constant guest,
 And our companion on the way.
 Fan our devotion's feeble flame;
 Let us press on to things before;
 Bring us together in Thy name
 Until we meet to part no more.

150 Tune, HENDON. 7s.

1 Come, my soul, thy suit prepare,
 Jesus loves to answer prayer,
 He himself has bid thee pray,
 Therefore will not say thee, nay.

2 Thou art coming to a King,
 Large petitions with thee bring,
 For His grace and power are such,
 None can ever ask too much.

151 Tune, STOCKWELL. 8s, 7s.

1 Blessed Bible, how I love it!
  How it doth my bosom cheer!
 What hath earth like this to covet?
  Oh, what stores of wealth are here!

2 'Tis a fountain ever bursting,
  Whence the weary may obtain
 Water for the soul that's thirsting,
  That it may not thirst again.

3 'Tis a chart that never faileth,
  One which God to man has given;
 And though oft the storm assaileth,
  It will guide you safe to heaven.

152 Tune, PLEYEL'S HYMN.

1 One with Christ! oh, blessed thought!
 We are by His spirit taught
 On His fulness now we live,
 Grace for grace we thence receive.

2 One with Christ! Ye saints, rejoice,
 As the objects of His choice;
 He will every want supply,
 While He lives we cannot die.

153 Tune, AMERICA.

1 Christ for the world we sing!
The world to Christ we bring
With loving zeal;
The poor, and them that mourn,
The faint and overborne,
Sin-sick and sorrow-worn,
Whom Christ doth heal.

2 Christ for the world we sing!
The world to Christ we bring
With fervent prayer;
The wayward and the lost,
By restless passions tost,
Redeemed at countless cost
From dark despair.

3 Christ for the world we sing!
The world to Christ we bring
With one accord;
With us the work to share,
With us reproach to dare,
With us the cross to bear,
For Christ our Lord!

154 Tune, WILMOT.

1 God is love; His mercy brightens
All the path in which we rove;
Bliss He wakes and woe He lightens;
God is wisdom, God is love.

2 E'en the hour that darkest seemeth,
Will His changeless goodness prove;
From the gloom His brightness stream-
eth:
God is wisdom, God is love.

3 He with earthly cares entwineth
Hope and comfort from above;
Everywhere His glory shineth:
God is wisdom, God is love.
Sir JOHN BOWRING.

155 Tune, WARD.

1 O Father, in these hallowed courts,
Withdrawn from every worldly care,
We humbly bow before Thy throne,
And turn to Thee in earnest prayer.

2 Thy quickening presence may we feel,
To light afresh the altar fires,
Till, in the glow of love divine,
Our souls shall burn with new desires!

3 Upon our hearts the burden roll:
The spirit of the Master give;
And may it be our highest joy,
Like Him, for others' good to live.

4 Inspire in all more fervent zeal
To send Thy glorious Word abroad,
Till, far and near, its cheering beams
Light every wanderer home to God!
W. F. SHERWIN. 1881.

156 Tune, PORTUGUESE HYMN.

O Father Almighty, to Thee be addrest,
With Christ and the Spirit, one God ever
blest, [heaven,
All glory and worship from earth and from
As was, and is now, and shall ever be given.

157 Tune, OLIVET.

1 My faith looks up to Thee,
Thou Lamb of Calvary,
Saviour divine!
Now hear me while I pray,
Take all my guilt away,
Oh, let me from this day
Be wholly Thine!

2 May Thy rich grace impart
Strength to my fainting heart;
My zeal inspire:
As Thou hast died for me,
Oh, may my love to Thee,
Pure, warm, and changeless be,
A living fire.

158 Tune, SHINING SHORE.

1 My days are gliding swiftly by,
And I, a pilgrim stranger,
Would not detain them as they fly!
Those hours of toil and danger.

CHORUS.

For oh! we stand on Jordan's strand,
Our friends are passing over,
And just before, the shining shore
We may almost discover.

2 We'll gird our loins, my brethren dear,
Our distant home discerning;
Our absent Lord has left us word,
Let every lamp be burning.

159 Tune, BOYLSTON.

1 Make haste, O man, to live,
For thou so soon must die;
Time hurries past thee like the breeze—
How swift its moments fly!

2 Make haste, O man, to do
Whatever must be done,
Thou hast no time to lose in sloth,
The day will soon be gone!

160   Tune, PLEYEL'S HYMN.

1 Christian brethren, ere we part,
Let us each, with grateful heart,
To our Father once more raise
Our united hymns of praise.

2 Here, perhaps, we meet no more,
But we seek a brighter shore,
Where, beyond all sin and pain,
Brethren, we shall meet again.

161   Tune, I AM SO GLAD.

1 Over the ocean, from lands far away,
Cometh the pleading of millions to-day;
"Send us the light of the gospel, we crave,
Tell us of Jesus, the Mighty to save."

CHORUS.

Hearken, O children, hear the sad cry
Coming to you, coming to you!
Surely the Lord will help, if you try
Something for Him to do!

2 Perishing thousands of children are there,
Having no Bible, or sermon, or prayer;
Fathers and mothers no Saviour have known,
Bowing to idols of wood and of stone.
Cho.—Hearken, O children, etc.

3 Gladly the children respond to the call,
Bringing their offerings — something from all;
Forming their Mission Bands, working with God;
Sending the news of salvation abroad.

CHO.—Come, then, O children, hasten to be
Earnest and true, earnest and true;
Tell the poor heathen, over the sea,
Jesus loves them and you.
                  W. F. SHERWIN. 1886.

162   Tune, WHAT A FRIEND.

1 Hark! the voice of Jesus calling,—
Who will go and work to-day?
Fields are white, the harvest waiting,—
Who will bear the sheaves away?
Loud and long the Master calleth,
Rich reward He offers free;
Who will answer, gladly saying,
"Here am I, O Lord, send me."

2 If you cannot cross the ocean
And the heathen lands explore,
You can find the heathen nearer,
You can help them at your door;
If you cannot speak like angels,
If you cannot preach like Paul,
You can tell the love of Jesus,
You can say He died for all.

3 While the souls of men are dying,
And the Master calls for you,
Let none hear you idly saying,
"There is nothing I can do!"
Gladly take the task He gives you,
Let His work your pleasure be;
Answer quickly when He calleth,
"Here am I, O Lord, send me."

163   Tune, WEBB.

1 Now be the gospel banner
In every land unfurled;
And be the shout,—"Hosanna!"
Re-echoed through the world;
Till every isle and nation,
Till every tribe and tongue,
Receive the great salvation,
And join the happy throng.

164   Tune, ROCKINGHAM.

Almighty God! Thy grace proclaim,
In every clime, of every name,
Till adverse powers before thee fall,
And crown the Saviour Lord of all!

165   Tune, MISSIONARY HYMN.

1 From Greenland's icy mountains,
From India's coral strand,
Where Afric's sunny fountains
Roll down their golden sand,—
From many an ancient river,
From many a palmy plain,
They call us to deliver
Their land from error's chain.

2 Shall we, whose souls are lighted
With wisdom from on high,—
Shall we, to men benighted,
The lamp of life deny?
Salvation, oh, salvation!
The joyful sound proclaim,
Till earth's remotest nation
Has learned Messiah's name.

3 Waft, waft, ye winds, His story,
And you, ye waters, roll,
Till, like a sea of glory,
It spreads from pole to pole;
Till o'er our ransomed nature
The Lamb for sinners slain,
Redeemer, King, Creator,
In bliss returns to reign!
                  R. HEBER.

166   Tune, BOYLSTON.

1 Come, kingdom of our God,
Sweet reign of light and love!
Shed peace and hope and joy abroad,
And wisdom from above.

2 Over our spirits first
Extend Thy healing reign;
There raise and quench the sacred thirst,
That never pains again!

3 Come, kingdom of our God!
And make the broad earth Thine;
Stretch o'er her lands and isles the rod
That flowers with grace divine.
                  H. B. JOHNS.

An Opening Service.

PREPARED BY W. F. SHERWIN.

OPENING HYMN.

SUPT. *Keep thy foot when thou goest to the house of God, and be more ready to heart han to give the sacrifice of fools: for they consider not that they do evil.*

RESPONSE. Let the words of my mouth, and the meditation of my heart, be acceptable in thy sight, O LORD, my strength, and my Redeemer.

S. *Offer unto God thanksgiving; and pay thy vows unto the Most High:*

R. Let us come before his presence with thanksgiving, and make a joyful noise unto him with psalms.

SELECTED HYMN.

S. *It is written, Man shall not live by bread alone, but by every word that proceedeth out of the mouth of God.*

R. The grass withereth, the flower fadeth: but the word of our God shall stand forever.

S. *If any of you lack wisdom, let him ask of God, that giveth to to all men liberally, and upbraideth not; and it shall be given him.*

R. Yea, if thou criest after knowledge, and liftest up thy voice for understanding; If thou seekest her as for silver, and searchest for her as for hid treasures:

S. *Then shalt thou understand the fear of the Lord, and find the knowledge of God.*

For the Lord giveth wisdom: out of his mouth cometh knowledge and understanding.

PRAYER.

TEACHERS. Now therefore, O our God, hear the prayer of thy servant, and his supplications, and cause thy face to shine upon thy sanctuary.

S. *So teach us to number our days, that we may apply our hearts unto wisdom.*

R. I will instruct thee and teach thee in the way which thou shalt go: I will guide thee with mine eye.

S. *That your faith should not stand in the wisdom of men, but in the power of God.*

R. But the wisdom that is from above is first pure, then peaceable, gentle, and easy to be entreated, full of mercy and good fruits, without partiality, and without hypocrisy.

S. *If thou be wise, thou shalt be wise for thyself: but if thou scornest, thou alone shalt bear it.*

R. They that be wise shall shine as the brightness of the firmament; and they that turn many to righteousness, as the stars for ever and ever.

(*Notices, Records, etc.,*)

STUDY SONG.

Read lesson and teach it.

Closing Service.

PREPARED BY W. F. SHERWIN.

SUPT. *Beloved, follow not that which is evil, but that which is good.*

RESPONSE. He that doeth good is of God: but he that doeth evil hath not seen God.

S. *Obey my voice, and I will be your God, and ye shall be my people: and walk ye in all the ways that I have commanded you, that it may be well unto you.*

Closing Service.

R. Thy word have I hid in mine heart, that I might not sin against thee.

S. Watch ye and pray, lest ye enter into temptation. The spirit truly is ready, but the flesh is weak.

R. For we wrestle not against flesh and blood, but against principalities, against powers, against the rulers of the darkness of this world, against spiritual wickedness in high places.

S. *Be ye doers of the word, and not hearers only, deceiving your own selves.*

R. If we walk in the light, as he is in the light, we have fellowship one with another, and the blood of Jesus Christ his Son cleanseth us from all sin.

S. *Blessed is the people that know the joyful sound: they shall walk, O Lord, in the light of thy countenance.*

R. I will behave myself wisely in a perfect way. I will walk within my house with a perfect heart.

CLOSING HYMN.

PRAYER.

S. *The Lord watch between me and thee, when we are absent one from another.*

R. God be merciful unto us, and bless us; and cause his face to shine upon us.

GLORIA PATRI. (*Page* 122.)

Salvation by Christ.

PREPARED BY EDW. H. SHERWIN.

HYMN.

SUPT. *For ye know the grace of our Lord Jesus Christ, that, though he was rich, yet for your sakes he became poor, that ye through his poverty might be rich.*

SCHOOL. For the son of man is come to seek and to save that which was lost.

SUPT. *For God sent not his Son into the world to condemn the world; but that the world through him might be saved.*

SCH. This is a faithful saying, and worthy of all acceptation, that Christ Jesus came into the world to save sinners.

SELECTED HYMN.

SUPT. *In that day there shall be a fountain opened to the house of David and to the inhabitants of Jerusalem for sin and for uncleanness.*

TEA. Jesus stood and cried, saying, If any man thirst, let him come unto me, and drink.

SCH. Whosoever drinketh of the water that I shall give him shall never thirst; but the water that I shall give him shall be in him a well of water springing up into everlasting life.

SUPT. *Whosoever will, let him take the water of life freely.*

TEA. Jesus said unto them, I am the bread of life: he that cometh to me shall never hunger; and he that believeth on me shall never thirst.

SCH. Him that cometh to me I will in no wise cast out.

SUPT. *For I came down from heaven, not to do mine own will, but the will of him that sent me.*

Salvation by Christ.

Tea. And this is the will of him that sent me, that every one which seeth the Son, and believeth on him, may have everlasting life: and I will raise him up at the last day.

Sch. Neither is there salvation in any other: for there is none other name under heaven given among men, whereby we must be saved.

SELECTED HYMN.

Supt. Come now and let us reason together, saith the Lord: though your sins be as scarlet, they shall be as white as snow; though they be red like crimson, they shall be as wool.

Tea. Repent ye therefore, and be converted, that your sins may be blotted out, when the times of refreshing shall come from the presence of the Lord.

Sch. If we confess our sins, he is faithful and just to forgive us our sins, and to cleanse us from all unrighteousness.

Supt. For thou, Lord, art good, and ready to forgive; and plenteous in mercy unto all them that call upon thee.

Tea. For God hath not appointed us to wrath, but to obtain salvation by our Lord Jesus Christ.

All. Jesus Christ the same yesterday, and to-day, and forever.

Faith.

Prepared by EDW. H. SHERWIN.

Supt. What is faith?

Sch. Faith is the substance of things hoped for, the evidence of things not seen.

Supt. What is the only source of faith?

Tea. Looking unto Jesus the author and finisher of our faith; who, for the joy that was set before him, endured the cross, despising the shame, and is set down at the right hand of the throne of God.

Supt. Does God require faith in us?

Sch. Without faith it is impossible to please him.

Supt. How can it be obtained?

Tea. Faith cometh by hearing, and hearing by the word of God.

Supt. Why should faith be found in the daily life?

Sch. The just shall live by faith.

Supt. How will it protect us?

Tea. Above all, taking the shield of faith, wherewith ye shall be able to quench all the fiery darts of the wicked.

Supt. What part should it have in prayer?

Sch. Let us draw near with a true heart in full assurance of faith.

Supt. Is it essential to victory?

Tea. And this is the victory that overcometh the world, even our faith.

Supt. Into what relation to God will it bring us?

Sch. For ye are all the children of God by faith in Christ Jesus.

Supt. Will faith alone save us?

Tea. Faith, if it hath not works, is dead, being alone. For as the body without the spirit is dead, so faith without works is dead also.

Supt. If faith is so essential, what should we do?

Sch. Examine yourselves, whether ye be in the faith; prove your own selves.

Faith.

SUPT. *Why should our faith be tested?*

TEA. That the trial of your faith, being much more precious than of gold that perisheth, though it be tried with fire, might be found unto praise, and honor, and glory, at the appearing of Jesus Christ.

SUPT. *How shall we prepare for such a test?*

SCH. Watch ye, stand fast in the faith, quit you like men, be strong.

SUPT. *What is the final outcome of faith?*

ALL. Blessed be the God and Father of our Lord Jesus Christ, who according to his abundant mercy, hath begotten us again unto a lively hope by the resurrection of Jesus Christ from the dead,

To an inheritance incorruptible, and undefiled, and that fadeth not away, reserved in heaven for you, who are kept by the power of God through faith unto salvation.

The Holy Spirit.

PREPARED BY E. H. SHERWIN.

SUPT. *The Holy Spirit is a person, not merely an influence.*

RESP. For there are three that bear record in heaven, the Father, the Word, and the Holy Ghost: and these three are one.

S. *Upon certain conditions we may enjoy His presence.*

R. If ye love me, keep my commandments. And I will pray the Father, and he shall give you another Comforter, that he may abide with you forever; even the Spirit of truth.

S. *Blasphemy against the Holy Spirit is the greatest of sins.*

R. Whosoever shall speak a word against the Son of man, it shall be forgiven him: but unto him that blasphemeth against the Holy Ghost it shall not be forgiven.

S. *By the spirit the holy scriptures were inspired.*

R. For the prophecy came not in old time by the will of man: but holy men of God spake as they were moved by the Holy Ghost.

S. *He reveals the truth to us.*

R. Howbeit when he, the Spirit of truth, is come, he will guide you into all truth:

He shall glorify me: for he shall receive of mine, and shall shew it unto you.

S. *He fills our hearts with love.*

R. The love of God is shed abroad in our hearts by the Holy Ghost which is given unto us.

S. *He helps us in our prayers.*

R. The spirit also helpeth our infirmities: for we know not what we should pray for as we ought: but the Spirit itself maketh intercession for us with groanings which cannot be uttered.

S. *By His help our prayers will prevail.*

R. And he that searcheth the hearts knoweth what is the mind of the Spirit, because he maketh intercession for the saints according to the will of God.

S. *The Holy Spirit leads us into communion with God.*

R. For as many as are led by the Spirit of God, they are the sons of God.

S. *He gives the assurance of this in our own hearts.*

R. The Spirit itself beareth witness with our spirit, that we are the children of God.

S. *It is open rebellion to resist the Holy Spirit.*

R. Ye stiffnecked and uncircumcised in heart and ears, ye do always resist the Holy Ghost: as your fathers did, so do ye.

S. *If we resist, he may leave us to our fate.*

R. And the Lord said, My Spirit shall not always strive with man

S. *What is the apostle's warning to those who have received the Holy Spirit?*

R. And grieve not the Holy Spirit of God, whereby ye are sealed unto the day of redemption.

Selected hymns may be interspersed at pleasure.

A Mission Service.

PREPARED BY W. F. SHERWIN.

SINGING.

Scripture lesson Isa. 60: 1-14. (or other selection.)

PRAYER.

SINGING.

QUESTION. *Why should we engage in mission work?*

ANS. Because Christ commands it.

Q. *What was his own great mission?*

A. The Spirit of the Lord is upon me, because he hath anointed me to preach the gospel to the poor; he hath sent me to heal the brokenhearted, to preach deliverance to the captives, and recovering of sight to the blind, to set at liberty them that are bruised,

To preach the acceptable year of the Lord. — Luke 4: 18. 19.

Q. *How did he fulfil this?*

A. And Jesus went about all Galilee, teaching in their synagogues, and preaching the gospel of the kingdom, and healing all manner of sickness and all manner of disease among the people. — Matt. 4: 23.

Q. *What was his last command to his disciples?*

A. And he said unto them, Go ye into all the world and preach the gospel to every creature — Mark 16: 15.

Q. *What special promise did he give with this?*

A. Lo, I am with you alway, even unto the end of the world. — Matt. 28: 20.

Q. *In what manner did they obey?*

A. And they went forth, and preached every where, the Lord working with them, and confirming the word with signs following. — Mark 16: 20.

Q. *Did the apostles confine this work to the Sabbath day?*

A. And daily in the temple, and in every house, they ceased not to teach and preach Jesus Christ. — Acts 5: 42

Q. *What was Paul's argument for sending out missionaries?*

A. For whosoever shall call upon the name of the Lord shall be saved. How then shall they call on him in whom they have not believed? and how shall they believe in him of whom they have not heard? and how shall they hear without a preacher? And how shall they preach, except they be sent? — Rom. 10: 13-15

Remarks, addresses and appropriate hymns may be introduced at pleasure.

INDEX.

Titles in Caps. First lines in Roman.

	NO.		NO.
A Cry comes over the Deep	105	Come to the Fountain	142
ADORATION	146	COME UNTO ME	56
After the Toil and Turmoil	125	Come with Gladness and with Singing	148
A GLORY GILDS THE PAGE	73	Come with Hearts and Voices now	154
Almighty God! Thy Grace proclaim	164	Come with thy Sins to the Fountain	142
ARE YOU COMING TO THE LIGHT?	35	CROSS OF CHRIST	80
ARE YOU WEARY?	41	Day is dying in the West	144
ARM OF THE LORD, AWAKE	23	Dear Friends and Brothers all	45
AROUND THE THRONE	78	DELAY NOT	68
Around the Throne of God	32	Don't think there is nothing for Children to do	79
AWAKE, MY SOUL	7		
AWAKE TO THE CONFLICT	112	ENTER HIS GATES	66
BEAUTIFUL BELLS OF THE MORN	31	EVEN AT THE DOOR	38
BEAUTIFUL HOME OF THE SOUL	60	EVENING PRAISE	144
Behold the Mighty King	21	FEAST OF THE KING	37
Blessed Lord, how much I need Thee	108	Fling out your Banner	28
Blessed Bible, how I love it!	150	FOR GOD AND DUTY	58
BLESS OUR SCHOOL TO-DAY	16	FOR THE TROUBLED WATERS	10
BLEST ARE THE PURE IN HEART	99	Friend of Sinners, hear my Plea	91
*BREAK THOU THE BREAD OF LIFE	30	From every stormy Wind	71
BUILD ON THE ROCK	46	GATHER THEM IN	4
CAST THY BURDEN ON THE LORD	64	Glad are the Notes	18
CHAUTAUQUA CLASS SONG, 1886	143	GLORIA	122
CHIEF OF SINNERS THOUGH I BE	100	Glory be to God on High	92
CHILD OF A KING	84	Glory be to the Father	122
CHILDREN, DO WHAT YOU CAN	79	Glory to God	94
CHILDREN'S DAY	107	GOD IS CALLING YET	29
Chime, sweet Bells	75	God is love; His Mercy brightens	152
CHRIST AROSE	103	God is my strong Salvation	57
Christ for the World we sing	151	GOD IS NEAR	85
Christ is calling us	58	Grant Thy Blessing, Lord	22
Christ is Knocking at my sad Heart	130	GUIDE ME, O THOU GREAT JEHOVAH	47
CHRIST, MY JOY	51	HAIL THE DAY	9
Christ, of all my Hopes	51	HAPPY LAND	121
CHRIST, OUR LORD, AROSE TO-DAY	36	HARK! HARK! MY SOUL	101
Christian Brethren, ere we part	159	Hark! the Church of Christ is calling	110
CHRISTMAS BELLS	75	Hark! the Voice of Jesus calling	102
CHRISTMAS CHIMES	133	Hasten, Lord, the glorious Time	86
Closing Hymn	97	HAVE YOU FALLEN?	12
Come into Christ's Army	70	HAVE YOU ANY ROOM FOR JESUS?	119
Come, my Soul, thy Suit prepare	149	Heavenly Gates are opened wide	133
COME TO JESUS	62	HE DIED FOR ME	82

(157)

INDEX.

	NO.		NO.
He's coming Soon	34	My Days are Gliding Swiftly by	157
Holy! Holy! Lord God Almighty!	1	My Father is rich	84
How Much I Need Thee	108	My Faith looks up to Thee	156
How Sweet to be allowed to Pray	102	My Home above	11
How Sweet to Pray	102	My Lord hath Ransomed me	98
I cast my Care on Thee	106	My strong Salvation	57
I have a Home	11	Nearer	113
I heard the Voice of Jesus say	56	No Room in thy Heart	52
I hear the Words of Jesus	132	Now be the Gospel Banner	163
I know not whether in Dreams of Night	4	O Christian, have you heard it?	34
		O Christ of God	147
I love to tell the Story	141	O Father Almighty, to Thee be addressed	155
I never knew you	130	
I open wide my Door	37	O Father, in these Hallowed Courts	160
I shall be Satisfied	128	O Jesus, I have Promised	120
I think, when I read	100	O Jesus, Thou art standing	83
I would be wholly Thine	104	O Lord, I Would Delight in Thee	106
I would Sing	19	O Sweet were the Words	54
In heavenly Love abiding	76	O welcome sweet Hour	13
In Him is Life	2	Oh! beautiful Home of the Soul	60
In His Name	118	Oh, come to the Lord with Rejoicing	111
In the Courts of Heaven	88	Oh, Could I Find, from Day to Day	55
Iott	67	Oh, do not let the Word Depart	70
Is your Lamp burning	127	Oh, for a Faith	48
Jerusalem, the Golden	126	Oh! I am so Happy in Jesus	2
Jesus all the Way	131	Oh, the Way was so Dreary	118
Jesus Christ is all my Song	8	Oh, Turn ye	90
Jesus, Lover of my Soul	15	Oh, we Love to Come	44
Jesus Only	20	Oh, worship the King	129
Jesus, Saviour, pilot me	117	Obeying Thy Divine Behest	148
Jesus, tender Saviour	16	One sweetly solemn Thought	3
Lead me, Saviour	120	One with Christ! Oh, blessed Tho't	153
Leaning on Jesus	53	Only Christ	8
Let us now, with Voice uplifted	49	On the Shoals	105
Light of Truth, so brightly shining	138	Onward, ever Onward	26
Like a River glorious	145	Opening Hymn	13
Like the One in Gospel Story	35	Open Thou our Eyes	137
Live, oh, live	43	Our parting Song of Praise	96
Live to serve the Master	43	Our Sabbath Home	44
Longing for Home	87	Over the Ocean, from Lands far away	161
Look and Live	25	Parting Song	96
Look to the Cross	25	Pass the Word along	110
Look, ye Saints	24	Redemption Song	98
Lord, I Desire with Thee to Live	55	Rejoice in Christ	50
Love Divine	39	Rest in Heaven	125
Make haste, O Man, to live	158	Return, O Wanderer	59
Marching on	61	Room for the Saviour	52
Morning breaks	40	Safely through another Week	77

(158)

INDEX.

Title	NO.
Salvation! Oh, the Joyful Sound.	74
Saviour, again to Thy dear Name	97
Saviour, like a Shepherd lead us.	115
Saviour, Pilot me	117
Saviour, when to Thee I Flee	42
Say, is your Lamp burning	127
Shall I let Him in?	130
Singing Glory	32
Sing of Christ	33
Sing once more	49
Softly fall the silver Moonbeams.	36
Soul of mine, in earthly Temple	128
Stowell	71
Sweet Land of Rest	87
Take the Banner of Salvation	138
Tarry by the Living Waters	72
Tarry not, my Brother	114
That Watchword is Love	70
The Accepted Time	114
The Bells of the joyous Morn	31
The Christian Banner	28
The Cleansing Fountain	134
The coming King is at the Door	38
The Gospel Call Obey	86
The Lord in His Temple Abideth.	111
The Lord's Day	5
The Master is Come	14
The Master's Call	14
The New Song	88
The Praise of the Children	63
The Prize is set before us	123
The Sweet Story of Old	100
There is a Fountain filled with Blood	134
There is a Happy Land	121
There is Joy among the Angels	135
There's a World of Love	39
They Sing of the Saviour above	63
'Tis Jesus, when the Burdened Heart.	131
To our Sabbath School	124
Triumph By-and-by	123
Trusting in Thee	91
Valiant Little Soldiers	27
Wake once more the Song	65
We are Fighting for our Freedom	81
We are Marching Gladly Onward	107
We are Marching Home	95
We are Marching on	81
We are Marching to that Heavenly Home	95
We Gather the Fragments	136
Weary with walking Alone	53
Welcome the Sabbath Hour	6
We'll Build on the Rock	46
We'll tarry by the Living Waters	72
What a Friend we have	140
What Can I Do for Jesus?	17
What Shall I Do for Christ?	93
When Friends thus Meet	45
When the King in His Beauty	139
When Sunbeams Gild my Way	113
When on Judea's Plains	94
When the Harvest is Past	116
When the Martyred One I see	82
When the Stars at set of Sun	85
While we we read Thy Holy Word	137
Wholly Thine	104
Who will Follow	21
Why not To-night?	69
Working, O Christ, with Thee	89
Working with Thee	89
Worthy of all Adoration	146
Yes, For me He careth	67

INDEX OF SUBJECTS.

ANNIVERSARY: 16-26-27-45-49-61-107-143.

ACTIVITY: 4-7-17-21-23-26-27-28-43-46-53-58-61-70-79-80-81-89-93-95-105-107-110-112-117-123-127-136-151-154-157-158-161-162-163-164.

AFFLICTION: 15-42-64-67-87-113-131-152.

BENEVOLENCE: 4-17-28-79-105.

BIBLE: 16-22-30-73-132-137-150.

CHRIST: { Birth of, 31-75-94-101-133. Death of, 80-82. Resurrection of, 18-36-40-65-103-147.

CONSECRATION: 15-17-21-29-33-37-47-51-53-55-82-83-89-91-102-104-106-109-113-120-127-128-134-147-149-152-156-157-158-160-162.

CLOSING: 69-89-96-97-116-122-144-155-158-159-164.

FAITH: 25-34-42-48-51-53-57-67-76-85-91-106-108-109-117-120-132-134-152-156.

HEAVEN: 3-11-26-30-60-78-87-88-95-121-125-126-135.

HOLY SPIRIT: 6-22-29-54-122.

HOPE: 10-76-113-132.

INVITATION: 10-12-14-25-29-35-37-41-52-56-59-61-62-68-69-90-114-116-119-130-132-134-139-142.

JOY, HYMNS OF: 2-7-9-11-19-24-26-27-31-32-33-34-40-44-45-49-51-63-66-72-74-84-88-95-101-103-107-110-111-121-123-126-135-141-143-146-147-151-153-154.

LORD'S DAY: 5-6-9-13-16-40-44-66-77-111-124-148.

LIFE AND DEATH: 3-38-64-113-152-157.

LOVE TO GOD: 55-84-99-152.

LOVE TO CHRIST: 2-5-8-14-15-16-17-19-20-32-36-37-42-53-64-70-82-83-89-91-93-100-104-106-109-115-120-130-131-140-141-147-148-153-156.

LOVE: 39-41-67-70-76-108.

MISSIONARY: 4-17-23-24-28-35-43-79-86-105-112-127-138-141-151-154-158-160-161-162-163-164.

OPENING: 1-5-6-7-13-16-30-33-44-49-66-73-77-92-102-108-111-124-129-137-140-143-146-148-149-150-153-154-156-160.

PRAYER: 13-16-22-25-47-64-71-102-106-108-120-124-137-140-148-149-156-160.

PRAISE TO GOD: 1-5-7-21-24-45-47-57-66-77-92-107-110-111-122-129-152.

PRAISE TO CHRIST: 2-8-11-19-20-23-32-33-34-38-40-46-50-51-52-56-63-78-80-88-92-98-101-118-119-122-123-129-131-132-133-134-146-147-151-156-163-164.

REPENTANCE: 10-15-25-29-35-37-41-59-82-83-109-114-116-130-132-134-135-156.

REST: 9-13-30-42-53-59-64-67-71-72-87-91-125-126-128-145.

SUNDAY SCHOOL: 4-16-21-22-27-30-44-45-49-63-66-78-89-107-124-150-161.

SALVATION: 2-8-10-14-19-25-29-32-33-35-37-41-46-52-62-69-72-74-90-98-114-118-119-130-134-135-138-139-142-151-163.

TEMPERANCE: 12-21-24-28-35-58-61-81-105-112-127-154.

WORSHIP: 1-7-9-13-15-16-22-33-47-63-66-71-77-89-92-97-102-104-106-108-111-113-117-122-124-129-140-144-146-147-148-149-152-153-155-156-160.

NOTE.— The hymn at opening of school may be of general praise or worship. It is especially desirable that the hymn *following* the lesson should be such as will at least tend to deepen rather than efface the impressions made. Sometimes the thoughtful selection of one or two verses will meet the want better than to sing the entire hymn. The above Index is made upon **the *general spirit* of** a hymn rather than its title.

www.ingramcontent.com/pod-product-compliance
Lightning Source LLC
Chambersburg PA
CBHW030304170426
43202CB00009B/859